THE TRUMP PHENOMENON &
THE EMERGENCE OF A NEW WORLD ORDER

Yash Tandon

THE TRUMP PHENOMENON &
THE EMERGENCE OF A NEW WORLD ORDER

Published by Zand Graphics Ltd.
PO Box 32843 – 00600, Nairobi
Email: zand.graphics@gmail.com

978-9966-10-379-6

First published in 2017
In collaboration with
FAHAMU
(Networks for Social Justice)
www.fahamu.rg

Printed, bound and distributed in the UK by
The African Books Collective (ABC Collective)
http://www.africanbookscollective.com/

Design and layout by
Henry Macharia

Contents

Acknowledgements

This little booklet owes its publication to comrades Zahid Rajan and Yves Niyiragira for the huge amount of work they have put into designing the layout and projection in its present shape and form. I thank my daughter, Nidhi, for editing and serialising the earlier incarnation of these papers in my blog, and to the editors of Pambazuka News for putting them out in what I regard as probably the best news and views periodical on Africa. I thank Roger van Zwanenberg – my literary agent - as well as several readers of these blogs (especially Riaz Tayob, Helene Bank, and Zarina Patel) for their comments that have helped me sharpen and nuance my arguments; and the Kenyan cartoonist 'Gado' for the use of his cartoons. His solidarity is much appreciated. Mary, my wife, I cannot thank enough. She was always the first to read the drafts which she subjected to both substantive and editorial scrutiny.

FOREWORD

I'm using the Trump Phenomenon as an "emblematic peg" to raise bigger issues of civilizational shift, and the strategy and tactics of struggle by peoples of the global North as well those of the global South. We need to assess what this phenomenon means for us in a cool, dispassionate and strategic manner.

Western civilization is in the autumn phase of its life

This civilization began with the slave trade 500 years ago. Slavery as a system has existed for thousands of years, but the "slave trade" – treating human beings as "commodities" - began in the period of Capitalism's "primitive accumulation". The Capitalist "civilization" has brought havoc to two-thirds of humanity, and to the environment. This civilization is in profound crisis. I analyse this at some length in my book *Trade is War*.[1]

Trump is a product of a failed system

I started writing my blogs on the US elections well before Trump's victory. On 20 September 2016 I put a question to myself: "Clinton or Trump: Who is a better bet for Africa?" I opted for Trump not because I like him, but I like Clinton even less.

In his election campaign Trump said distasteful things about the Muslims, immigrants, Mexicans, women, Africans - among others. But Trump was (and is) unpredictable. Clinton was totally predictable: she is for war. She was the Establishment candidate from day zero, a child of the "deep state". Trump is a trader: he could trade for peace with Russia. He spewed fire over Iran and China (and still does so), but he could be tamed. Clinton is untamable; she was gung-ho over war.[2] There were other reasons for opting for Trump. He had said nasty things about Africa, but he had also criticised the notion of "exporting democracy" to Africa: "It is not American business to tell Africa how to run their countries." I can live with that. We in Africa (or the rest of the global South) cannot accept the "regime change" interventionist policies of America and Europe.

Trump defeated 16 well-placed Republican candidates in the primaries, and then went on to defeat Clinton to become President. He came under a lot of criticism from the American deep state and the Establishment media. This was predictable. So Trump took to twitting - a brilliant tactical resort to contemporary means of mass communication.

Who is this guy? Why has he succeeded against enormous odds? This booklet will go into some of these questions. But I will say only one word here. Trump won partly because of his own skills, but mainly because the world is changing.

Incompatibility between capitalism and democracy

Before we understand the nature of this shift, we need to understand the world we live in - *In Part Six - What is Fascism in our Times?* - I go into this in some detail. Except for some enlightened historians like Karl Polanyi, philosophers like Jürgen Habermas, and journalists like Chris Hedges, the West is caught up in a historical trap from which its people (including the intelligentsia) are unable to escape. The result is that they have not much to offer in order for us to understand the essential nature of our times. Polanyi understood this well back in the 1940s. He wrote: "*Fascism is born from the incompatibility between democracy and capitalism in a fully developed industrial society. Either capitalism or democracy must therefore disappear. Fascism constitutes the solution to this deadlock by allowing capitalism to persist.*"

THE TRUMP PHENOMENON & THE EMERGENCE OF A NEW WORLD ORDER

Trump won the "democratic" election. Did he really?

If he did, it begs the question: what is democracy? Western countries claim to be "democratic". But they are not. The system is "fascist". It's a systemic, structural, phenomenon, not personal. The person (Trump) becomes the most visible carrier of a fascist project. As Polanyi explained, fascism is a necessary product of capitalism-imperialism seeking to get out of its deepening crisis. The World Trade Organisation (WTO) - an organisation I well know from first-hand experience - is the Empire's last stage by the economic means. The WTO is a fascist project; its success will result in nothing less than the globalization of fascism. Fortunately, the WTO is facing relentless challenges from the nations of the global South.

Trump, the anti-establishment proto-nationalist

What interested me is that Trump is not part of the American "Establishment". The US Establishment is at the core of the global imperial system. What also interested me about Trump is that he is a nationalist – in his own way. Nationalism is a phenomenon that the Western "liberal-left" media and intelligentsia do not understand. Why not? It is because they look at it from an essentially Eurocentric perspective. In Part Two: "Imperialism and Revolution", and Part Three: "Capitalism and Economic Nationalism", I analyse the significance of the National Question (NQ) at some length. The NQ goes back to Lenin's 1913 *"Thesis on the National Question"*, but it is missing from the vocabulary of contemporary Western "Marxists". For them nationalism is a regressive, backward, force. In Part Seven: Politics of Resistance and Solidarity, I describe two kinds of nationalisms - one offensive and the other defensive. The South's struggle against the global imperial system is quintessentially defensive.

Don't get me wrong – Trump is no Marxist, nor has he read Lenin's thesis. But, as I said, he is a nationalist "in his own way". He wants to bring industries back to America and create jobs for Americans. Whether he succeeds or not is a different matter. But it is significant that one of his first executive directives was to tear up the TPP (Trans Pacific Partnership) Agreement.

The "left" in Europe and America is very different from the "left" in the global South. Western "left-liberals" have joined with their ruling classes to applaud "globalisation" … erroneously identified with "internationalism". The two are very different, and I explain this in part three.

PART ONE

TRUMP AND TRUMPISM

Trump's electoral victory is a good reason to reflect on a whole range of bigger issues that have been crowded out by the ear-splitting anti-Trump campaigns in America and liberal-left circles in Europe. The hysteria, no doubt, is a passing phenomenon. Some diehards will continue, but the rest will settle down to the demands of routine existence. Trump is a reality firmly embedded in the American political landscape.

Trump and Trumpism

Trump is an avant-garde – unconventional but also, in some odd ways, innovative. To my knowledge there has never been a phenomenon like him in American political history – somebody who not only defeated all his Republican rivals in the primaries, but also told his Party to go fishing whilst he prepared – without any real experience in government – to challenge the Democratic candidate.

Trump is, of course, not my kind of person. I do not share many of his values, and I find his language offensive and demeaning. He is described by his detractors as racist, homophobic, xenophobic, misogynist, and much else besides. I think these are exaggerated adjectives, but I understand where they come from, given the political climate and the degeneration of American democracy. It is difficult to say how much of these were expressions of Trump's generally macho personality and "locker-room" talk.[3] in order to attract media attention. Trump had a running feud with the mainstream media, but the latter could not take their eyes off him. He is a dramatist *par excellence*. Hillary Clinton was simply no match.

Trump is a capitalist, albeit a self-made capitalist; but he is not part of the Establishment. Even Bernie Sanders in the US and Jeremy Corbyn in the UK recognise this.[4] He was fighting the Establishment which was pre-structured against him right from ground zero. Trump is a "nationalist"; his campaigning slogan was: "Make America Great Again!" I am an internationalist (not globaliser), but I am also a nationalist – "Restore Africa's dignity and self-reliance". But Trump and I represent different strands of nationalism.

If Trump defies the World Trade Organisation (WTO) and introduces protection for local American industries to create jobs, then he is on the side of my kind of nationalism. One of his acts on assuming power was to throw into the dust-bin the Obama-initiated TPP (Trans Pacific Partnership). He might do the same with the TTIP (Transatlantic Trade and Investment Partnership), in line with his opposition to the European Union.[5]

He might also scrap the American Growth and Opportunities Act (AGOA), which has been divisive of Africa; and Obama's "Power Africa" $7 billion initiative. That's good too. These "initiatives" of Obama were to help corporate America, not Africa. If Trump talks with Russia, China, Iran and Syria, and defies Clinton's war-mongering, then he could help forces of peace and reconciliation that the world badly needs.

Trump does not have Africa on his map. He has criticised the notion of "exporting democracy"; it is not his business, he says, to tell Africans how to run their countries. That's good. We in Africa need allies, yes, but we do not need the Anglo-American Empire or Europe to tell us how to run our countries. Yes, we have problems – and these arise from centuries of exploitation and oppression, from the days of slave trade to today's so-called globalisation. Yes, we have our share of corruption, leadership problems, divided communities, and civil wars. But we also have Ubuntu, humanist, values. Africans are divided, but pan-Africanism vibrates strongly in the heart of all Africans. So, leave us alone; we'll sort out our problems.

PART TWO

IMPERIALISM AND REVOLUTION

Western denial of the reality of imperialism

People in the West, including well-meaning NGOs and people otherwise sympathetic to Africa, have difficulty recognizing the reality of imperialism. In my book, *Trade is War*, I wrote this:

> I have sought to find an explanation in both Western culture and history to illuminate this mental blockage, but I have not come up with a good answer. ... I have often wondered why Hitler is described in almost all Western literature as a "fascist" but never as an imperialist. Could it be that calling Hitler an imperialist is too perilously close to looking at a mirror image? Today, many Westerners, including intellectuals, deny the existence of imperialism.[6]

In the book I related my experience at a conference I attended in November 1995, in Maastricht, Netherlands. I was engaged in a public debate with Herman Cohen, a former US Under-Secretary of State for African Affairs. The debate was on "democracy and governance" in Africa. When I used the word "imperialism" to describe the situation in Africa, Cohen countered by saying I was "anachronistic", and that imperialism was simply "a figment of Tandon's imagination". I did not have to answer him; Africans amongst the audience gave him several concrete examples of imperialism. Among them was Aminata Traoré, a Malian writer and political activist. Cohen was unmoved, his mind blocked by a serious case of what I call Intransigent Imperialism Rejection Syndrome (IIRS).

So for those that suffer from IIRS, let me define imperialism. Imperialism is a particular kind of relationship that arose in the wake of 19-20th century colonialism. It may not be reduced to any kind of asymmetrical power relationship. Could the relations between the USA and Europe, for example, be described also as imperialist? No. Why not? Because although they have unequal power, at the global level they are both imperialist powers - partners and competitors perpetrating the same crime. They compete and collaborate to maintain a system of production and consumption based on the exploitation of the rich resources – including labour and environment – of the South. Imperialism is a concrete, existential, phenomenon. It cannot be simply wished away by a rude dismissive gesture of your hands – as Cohen did to me at Maastricht.

Imperialism's sanitised version – Free Trade Globalisation (FTG)

During the last thirty years – to be precise, during the reign of Thatcher in the UK and Reagan in the US – a sanitised version of imperialism has appeared. It is called *Free Trade Globalisation*. In fact, it has gone beyond the 19th - 20th Century reality of imperialism. It is presented as a "scientific truth" - like gravity: nobody can escape the gravitational pull of FTG; in fact, they say it is a good thing!

Theresa May, in her first foreign policy speech at London Lord Mayor's banquet on 14 November 2016, promised to "make globalisation work for all". It has "left behind" too many people, she said. In the Post-Brexit period, Britain has a "historic" opportunity to take on "a new role as the global champion of free trade."[7] So for Theresa May – indeed like all deniers of the reality of imperialism - FTG is like gravity. It has become the Empire's new liturgy.

Later, in Part 6, we will show that FTG is not irresistible; there is nothing "scientific" about it. In the book *Trade is War* I show that there has never, ever, been something called "free trade" since the rise of capitalism circa 500 years ago.

Clinton versus Trump: who is the imperialist ideologist?

The answer is clear: Clinton is the imperialist jingoist. Under her as Secretary of State, the US - and the North Atlantic Treaty Organisation (NATO) - went to war against Libya, well beyond the mandate of the UN Security Council. The end of the war was the gruesome death of Gaddafi cornered in a hell-hole. Clinton, on viewing this on the screen, remarked with mocking, derisive laughter: "We came, we saw, he died".

In his *"Inside the Invisible Government: War, Propaganda, Clinton and Trump"* [8]John Pilger writes:

> In 2011, Libya ... was destroyed on the pretext that Muammar Gaddafi was about to commit genocide on his own people. That was the

incessant news; and there was no evidence. It was a lie. In fact, Britain, Europe and the United States wanted what they like to call "regime change" in Libya, the biggest oil producer in Africa. Gaddafi's influence in the continent and, above all, his independence were intolerable. So he was murdered with a knife in his rear by fanatics, backed by America, Britain and France. ... According to its own records, NATO launched 9,700 "strike sorties" ... They included missiles with uranium warheads. ... [Look at] the mass graves identified by the Red Cross. The UNICEF report on the children killed says, "most [of them] under the age of ten".

As a direct consequence, Sirte became the capital of ISIS. To the militarists in Washington, the real problem with Trump is that, in his lucid moments, he seems not to want a war with Russia; he wants to talk with the Russian president, not fight him; he says he wants to talk with the president of China.

Good nationalism, Bad nationalism

Most "left-liberal" organisations in Europe come from a strong internationalist background and socialist ideology. They regularly identify nationalism with fascism or neo-fascism. Why, one might ask, is "socialism" acceptable but not "nationalism"? What's wrong with nationalism?[9]

Nationalism is not too much of a problem in the United States, where they celebrate it with passion. 240 years ago the thirteen American colonies declared independence from England – an event celebrated on July 4 every year. But what is ironic (hypocritical?) is that nationalism is acceptable for the white Americans, not for the (coloured) Latinos, Africans and Asians. Nationalism is good for America, bad for the global South.

There is an interesting difference here between the US and Europe. In Europe there is general hostility against nationalism – prominently amongst the "left-liberals", but NOT amongst the "right". In America, on the other hand, there is hostility against (and only against) third world nationalism cutting across the left-right political divide. Why?

Let me offer an explanation.

In Western Europe anti-nationalism has, essentially, two sources. One is the experience of "national socialism" under Hitler. Since then socialism was rescued, but nationalism became a dirty word. The second is the experience of the Second World War which had its origins in Europe. One of the arguments

THE TRUMP PHENOMENON & THE EMERGENCE OF A NEW WORLD ORDER

against Brexit (Britain exiting the EU) was that the European Union has been a strong deterrent against another intra-European war, and against the resurgence of nationalism.

In Europe, thus, there is a palpable alarm in "left-liberal" circles about nationalism's resurgence, often equated with "neo-fascism" or "populism" – or both. In recent years we have seen the rise of the *National Front* in France, the *Party for Freedom* in the Netherlands, the *Danish People's Party* in Denmark, the *Progress Party* in Norway, and the *UK Independence Party* (UKIP). Many of these parties rejoiced at the UK's Brexit vote, hailing it as a triumph for their own nationalist positions. Not surprisingly, they also hailed Trump's victory.

There is a third reason. And this is shared by the "liberal-left" Americans and Europeans alike. This reason is Russia. Russia is often singled out in the Western mainstream media for its nationalism. For example, on 20 November 2014 the (London) *Economist* carried an article entitled: "*Nationalism is back*". The writer argued, "The most serious threat to the stability of Europe … remains Russian nationalism. The biggest security question facing Europe— and perhaps the world—will be whether President Putin rides the nationalist wave he has helped to create, and continues to threaten Ukraine and even the Baltic states."[10]

In the US, Trump has no problem with Russia or Putin. Hillary Clinton cannot stand Putin. "We have 17 intelligence agencies, civilian and military", she said, "who have all concluded that these espionage attacks, these cyber-attacks, come from the highest levels of the Kremlin, and they are designed to influence our election."[11]

The Essence of Fascism

One of the most insightful analysts of fascism was the economic historian Karl Polanyi, author of the classic *"The Great Transformation"*. He described the link between global capital and state power as "Globalised Fascism" - way before the rest of us began to talk about globalisation in the post-1980s era. Polanyi witnessed the rise of fascism and devoted much effort to understand it in order to better fight it. As he put it: "After the abolition of the political democratic sphere, economic life alone remains; capitalism as organised in the different sectors of industry becomes the whole of society. It is the fascist solution."[12]

For a more contemporary understanding of this phenomenon, see: Samir Amin, *The Return of Fascism in Contemporary Capitalism*, Monthly Review, 2014.

The National Question

As I said earlier, the "left-liberal" in Europe and America do not recognise the National Question. It is missing, for example, in an otherwise excellent study called "*The Communist Manifesto: A Weapon of War*" by Doug Enaa Greene. He says: "Despite being written over 160 years ago, the Communist Manifesto remains as relevant as ever."[13] However, there is no mention of the National Question. Greene chose to ignore a debate that goes back (under various formulations) in the writings of Marx, Lenin, Rosa Luxemburg, Mao, Castro ... and in more recent times, Dani Wadada Nabudere, Samir Amin and other Marxist revolutionaries.

In a debate with Patrick Bond in 2014 I argued against his thesis that the BRICS (Brazil, Russia, India, China and South Africa) are "sub-imperialist" countries. This arises, I argued, from Bond's non-recognition or inadequate understanding of the National Question.[14] I will not get into that debate here. I will simply refer readers to further analysis of the National Question in two books. One is *Reclaiming the Nation: The Return of the National Question in Africa, Asia and Latin America* (2011) edited by Sam Moyo and Paris Yeros (Pluto Press); and the other is *Nationalism and National Projects in Southern Africa: New Critical Reflections* (2013), edited by Sabelo J. Ndlovu-Gatsheni and Fenix Ndhlovu, especially Part Four on "National Question, Ethnicity and Citizenship".

Summary and conclusions

1. Imperialism is an existential reality in our times. Western denial of it arises out of what I call the Intransigent Imperialism Rejection Syndrome (IIRS).

2. Today imperialism exists in its sanitised version –it is called "Free Trade Globalisation" (FTG)

3. Between Hillary Clinton and Donald Trump, evidence shows clearly that it is Clinton who is the imperialist ideologist.

4. For the American and European "left-liberal", socialism is acceptable but not nationalism (except if you are a white American and celebrate the 4th of July every year).

5. In Europe, following the massive influx of refugees from the Middle East and Africa (a product mainly of Western imperialist interventionist foreign policy in Iraq, Libya, Syria, and other places), there is a resurgence of nationalism, often equated with "neo-fascism" or "populism"- or both.

6.   Fascism has deeper roots. As Polanyi explained, there is a symbiotic link between global capital and state power reproduced as "Globalised Fascism".

7.   The Western "left-liberal" political elite, academia, and the media have a blind spot that obliterates the National Question from their vision. Unlike nationalism in the West which turns aggressive under imperialism, nationalism in the global South is defensive, and is aimed at completing the struggle for national independence from "globalised fascism".

PART THREE

CAPITALISM AND ECONOMIC NATIONALISM

Introduction

Capitalism has been a progressive force in its times. But it has given rise to resistance at various levels. The first resistance came from its exploited classes – the industrial workers. When Capitalism was obliged - by its own logic - to colonise, it gave rise to national resistance. Hence we had the American war of independence in the 19th century, and wars and struggles for national independence in the global south in the 20th … and still continuing.

This struggle has both a political and an economic dimension. This segment deals with the economic. In the previous segment, under the sub-heading "the National Question", we dealt with its essentially political and ideological dimension.

Economic nationalism is part of the liberation struggle against imperialism. It is my contention that students of "economics" need a higher degree of awareness of history and a deeper understanding of the geopolitics of economic nationalism in order to make sense of the economic and political realities on the ground.

Economic nationalism is a universal phenomenon

We'll start with the very continents that are today opposed – ideologically – to economic nationalism, namely the United States and the European Union. However, what they preach is not what they do, or wish to do. They are as much economic nationalists as the very countries they criticise. The evidence of this proposition is overwhelming – from agriculture to the environment to banking. Let us take banking and finance. It is arguably the most "international" in character.

In Europe the banks are facing a serious crisis as a result of tough competition from American Banks. European investment banks are losing out market share to Americans. Germany's biggest Bank, Deutsch Bank, has acknowledged that it must retreat from "global" ambitions, following €6 bn. quarterly loss, 9000 jobs cuts (a quarter of workforce). Top European Bankers, which includes the Chairman of Barclays, John McFarlane, have warned of the American threat to their future. France's Société Générale Chief Executive Frederic Qudea and president of European Banking Federation said that a handful of "robust" American banks "are gaining market share abroad while strengthening their positions at home". He said that the top 5 US banks had increased their share of the global capital market from 48 to 59 percent in past 5 years, while the top 5 EU banks have slipped from 35 to 31 percent. [15]

Other examples of economic nationalism

In April 2005, the US company Chevron and the China National Offshore Oil Corp (CNOOC) made competitive bids for Unocal, a Californian oil company. The ferocious reaction of the Congress against the Chinese bid surprised nobody, except those deluded by the ideology of free flow of capital across borders. The Congress feared that the Chinese takeover would put to risk American energy sovereignty and compromise its "national security". [16]

In July 2005, the French political elite mounted a massive campaign to prevent Danone, the country's leading food group, against takeover by an American "predator" - PepsiCo. How could, they said, the US dare take over "our national champion". [17]

Western duplicity over the issue of economic nationalism

Of course, it is different story if a "third world" country dares to exercise economic nationalism.

In April 2012, Argentina's President Christina Kirchner asked Congress, in the interest of securing "hydrocarbon self-sufficiency", to nationalise oil and gas producer YPF, owned largely by the Spanish conglomerate Repsol YPF – a company that employs 24,000 workers globally and has revenue of EUR 44.67 (2014). She also took action against other hedge funds. The Western reaction was strong: how dare a "communist third world banana republic" take matters in its hands like this? Following smear campaigns, street wars between the embattled Kirchner and the "deep State" backed by the Empire, Kirchner lost her Presidency. In February 2016, the new President, Mauricio Macri, offered to pay $6.5 billion to the group of six hedge fund holdouts. In addition to the 75% payment in principal and hefty interest accumulated over the years, thirteen years of hefty legal bills would also be picked up by Argentina. Estimates on the returns that the "super holdouts" will make on their investment in Argentina's bonds range from three to five times what they had paid for the bonds.[18]

Resource nationalism

All the three cases described above relate to resource nationalism. Global resources are unequally distributed, the bulk of them are in the global South. Their ownership and control, however, remain largely in the hands of Western corporations which are jealously protecting their "historical rights" over these resources.[19]

This is a very sensitive area of the struggle between the global North and the global South. Obviously, we cannot even begin to make a list of the many issues involved. However, I would like to mention two that are often either left out of mainstream research or dealt with rather cursorily.

One is the issue of the rights of indigenous peoples the world over. These can no longer be ignored. They are the battle-lines of the future. What we see in Bolivia, Ecuador, Venezuela...are the beginnings of "Arab Spring" in the area of natural resources, and will spread over the rest of the world - not least, Canada, Australia, New Zealand, and most of Asia and Africa.

The second is the issue of women's rights to natural resources. At the international level, the "national" rights to the resources are a burning issue. But at the national and local levels, it is the right of women to these resources that is critical, especially land. In fact, land and women's rights are two sides of the same coin. Metaphorically, land is women, and women are land. (I know this from my 15 years' experience working amongst the rural people in southern Africa).

The ideological terrain

Here the battle lines go back to the "free trade" versus "protection" debate. *It is largely an academic, ideological, debate,* for, as we have seen above, economic nationalism (including protectionism) is a universal phenomenon. There is nothing called "free trade".

A bit of history will give a proper context to this debate.

The American 1775-1783 war against England was about economic (as well as, of course, political) independence. Following independence, America went for a full-fledged program of economic nationalism. Within 50 years, the US was well on its way to industrialisation. Friedrich List, a German political-economist, then living in the United States, decided he could suggest to his compatriots that they, too, should follow the lead of the US. In 1841 he wrote *The National System of Political Economy.* It was the beginning of economic nationalism in Germany, followed by other countries in Europe and then Japan.

In 1884-5, the European nations met in Berlin and carved up Africa. The German Chancellor Bismarck presided over the division. The Europeans needed access to cheap raw materials which they could no longer get from America or the older colonies. This was the material reality. The erstwhile economic nationalists turned imperialist. It is only one step from being a "nationalist" to being an "imperialist". Germany needed colonies for the sake of "national" interest.

None of the past economic theories - classical, neoclassical, Listian, German historical school, Austrian school, among others (nor their contemporary advocates) - came to save Africa from savage colonisation. Not even, for that matter, did the Hamilton School of American nationalists. Why not? The reason is clear: at the time, the Americans were preoccupied with their own imperialist project in South America declaring these as their "sphere of interest" under the Monroe Doctrine. New theories (ideologies) had to be invented to legitimise Africa's predation. Economic theories were now embellished by a missionary ideology - "the white man's burden" to "civilize" the rest of the world.

Today, as we discussed above, it is "free trade globalisation". My *Trade is War* gives a blow by blow account and analysis of this Empire-driven curious phenomenon of "free trade" that belies reality on the ground.[20]

The way forward

1. The first thing we must realise is that this is an upstream struggle. The Empire is not about to disappear any time soon. For sure, it is weakening, and for all intents and purposes, it has become a "paper tiger". But it still has a lot of clout to do an enormous damage to the rest of the world. To get some insight into this, look at what has been happening to Greece over the last few years.[21]

2. The following are some of the highlights of the way forward. I have Africa in mind, but they have relevance for the whole of the global South.

3. We need to challenge the economic orthodoxy, and work on development alternatives that take into account the fact that all countries – without exception – are economic nationalists, including those that swear by the ideology of "free market globalisation".[22]

4. One of the most vital aspects on an alternative strategy is to protect local industries that add value to local resources, and put in place strong barriers against imports that kill local industries. I know this goes against the so-called "laws" of the World Trade Organisation (WTO). So be it. Let the WTO and the Empire impose sanctions on Africa. They cannot harm African economies more than they are already doing. Decoupling from "free market globalisation" must be properly strategized and sequenced. The "value addition" must be done first at the local level, then at the national level, then regional and continental.

5. There should be no "open door" policy towards "free trade" and Foreign Direct Investments (FDIs) in general. These might be allowed as and when required by national consensus between the Government, the local (not foreign) private sector, the workers, small farmers, and other organs of civil society. The FDIs must operate under certain nationally determined conditions (for example, limited access to domestic

savings), and they must conform to certain performance requirements (for example, effective transfer of technology and managerial know-how).

6. Economic nationalism does not preclude regionalism – nations getting together to integrate regionally. In fact, for Africa to get rid of the yoke of European and American imperialism it is imperative that they integrate at a continental level, though starting, at first, at regional level as prescribed by, for example, the Lagos Plan of Action that the African Union agreed to in April 1980 – a plan that was systematically subverted by the World Bank, acting for the Empire.

PART FOUR

THE DEEP STATE & THE IMPERIAL ESTABLISHMENT

There is widespread hearsay that with Donald Trump all bets are off. Anything can happen. The man is unpredictable.

Trump's assumption of power could be the beginning of a sea change in America's relations with the rest of the world. But, and this is important for us to understand that it is not up to him, or to America, even if the USA is militarily and economically the most powerful country in the world. We should bear in mind that there are always some enduring features embedded in the structures of our economies and global geopolitics.

Let us make a poised assessment of what difference Trump would make.

What difference would Trump make?

As a presidential candidate Trump had said a lot of outrageous things. Equally, much of the political "left-liberals" in Europe and America reacted with what

can only be described as hysteric panic attack. They said Trump will round up Muslims and Mexicans and put them in jail together with Hillary Clinton; encourage the Ku Klux Klan to return to the old days of slavery; unleash mass repression of women and LGBTs; abolish the health care; endanger the planet with his cavalier attitude towards the environment, and with his finger on the nuclear button; appoint his racist and anti-Semitic friends in his cabinet; and bring an apocalyptic extinction of the liberal world order. A sensational knockout!

Among those who made a more balanced appraisal was, for example, the essay by Professors David Held and Kyle McNally: *"Gold Plated Populism: Trump and the end of the Liberal Order"*:[23]

> Donald Trump's electoral victory has startled the world. It seems to usher in an era marked by the triumph of fear and anger, brazen disregard for reason and truth, the weakening hold of liberalism, the fracturing of the postwar consensus, and the rolling back of gains made from an integrated world economy. On the horizon, by contrast, is protectionism, wall building, and deeply exclusionary practice.

Held and McNally go on then to say this:

> Yet, little of this is Trump's invention or design. The post-war order has shown cracks for many years; regional and international institutions have been weakened steadily; nationalism and xenophobia have been on the rise; militant and intolerant discourses have spread like wildfire and authoritarian populism has emerged across many parts of the world. The roots of this are deep and extensive.

Where does President Trump fit in all this? Well, he appears to have sobered up, he has pulled back some of his punches, whilst still standing firmly on some other issues. For example, in an interview with the *New York Times*[24], Trump is reported to have said the following among other things:

1.   He has dropped the idea of jailing Hillary Clinton.
2.   On climate, he said: "I have an open mind to it", and that clean air and "crystal clear water" are vitally important.
3.   He said the Iraq war was "one of the great mistakes in the history of our country", but he has "very definitive" and "strong ideas" about how to deal with the violent civil war raging in Syria.
4.   He said it would be "nice" if he and President Putin could get along, but he rejected the idea that any warming of relations would be called a "reset", noting the criticism that Clinton received after her attempts to "reset" relations with Russia had failed.

On the other hand, he defended his Cabinet appointments like Stephen Bannon as his chief strategist,[25] and James Mattis as his Secretary of Defence. He also defended the appointment of his son-in-law, Jared Kushner as "Senior Adviser". He said he had no "legal obligation" to establish boundaries between his business empire and his White House. Later he elaborated to say that he would distance himself from his businesses, and that his "great business" is to focus on the Presidency.[26]

Bannon came to Hollywood with ideas from the concept of dharma in Baghvat Gita, Arthur Conan Doyle, Nietsche, Madame Blavatshy, Ramkrishna, Baal Shem, and Geroniuro. He is willing to break with authority and thinks big, excited by grand theories.

So the future is still largely open-ended. Trump could try to make a difference, but whether he would succeed or not depends on many systemic and structural constraints at both national and global levels.

The deep state and the imperial establishment

Among a section of the left in Europe and America there is scant understanding of the phenomenon of "the Establishment". In my earlier piece I gave its definition and history which is worth summarising. I traced it down to the creation of the British Empire towards the turn of the 19th Century, and associated with names like Cecil Rhodes, Alfred Milner, Lionel Curtis, Robert

Brand and Adam Marris. A part of their strategy was to deliberately provoke wars - such as those leading to the British colonisation of South Africa. This is "the Establishment". Rhodes died in 1902, but the Anglo-American Establishment lives on and has mutated over time. Now it is represented by the global corporations that effectively control the world's major resources (gold, diamonds, oil, etc.), banks including financial services, and the institutions of global governance (such as the IMF, the World Bank and the World Trade Organisation).

Others have referred to this as "the Deep State" - or state within state - which controls policy irrespective of what political party is in power. In the next segment we analyse the military-industrial-financial complex in the US as an essential part of the Establishment. But there are other aspects which are as potent as the military industrial complex. These include the academia (about which I will write another time), and the media.

The media as part of the deep state

The well-known investigative journalist, John Pilger, has a good description of the media as part of the "deep state" in his "*Inside the Invisible Government: War, Propaganda, Clinton and Trump*".[27] He said, the Western media such as the BBC, NBC, CBS, and the CNN, and "liberal" newspapers like the *Washington Post, the Guardian*, and *the Economist*, present themselves as "… enlightened, progressive tribunes of the moral zeitgeist - anti-racist, pro-feminist and pro-LGBT. And they love war".

Pilger cites Ukraine as "media triumph" in conditioning viewers and readers to accept a new cold war. Russia is maligned when, in fact, the 2014 coup in Ukraine was the work of the American intelligence establishment. Once again, it is "… the Ruskies are coming to get us, led by another Stalin, whom *The Economist* depicts as the devil". There is a systematic suppression of truth about Ukraine. It is, says Pilger, "one of the most complete news blackouts I can remember." There is an all-pervasive "media *joie d'esprit* - a class reunion of warmongers … inciting war with Russia".

Truth, says Pliger, is engineered. Human Rights don't matter. The human rights record of Saddam Hussein or Gaddafi was just a ruse; they were irrelevant. The truth is that they did not obey orders from the USA and Britain and surrender their countries to the Empire. So they took matters in their own hands without a mandate from the UN Security Council, attacked Iraq and Libya, and murdered Sadaam and Gaddafi. The former British Foreign Office official, Carne Ross, who was responsible for operating sanctions against Iraq, told Pilger: "We would feed journalists factoids of sanitised intelligence, or we would freeze them out. That is how it worked." Had journalists told the truth, the attack on Iraq would not have happened; hundreds of thousands of men, women and children would be alive today.

When the terrorists attacked parts of Paris in November 2015, President Francoise Hollande immediately sent planes to bomb Syria – and, predictably, more terrorism followed - the product, says Pilger, "of Hollande's bombast about France being 'at war' and 'showing no mercy'. That state violence and jihadist violence feed off each other is the truth that no national leader has the courage to speak," says Pilger.

And, I might add, the West's attack on Iraq, Libya, and Syria - this "war without mercy"- is the root cause of the massive exodus of refugees to Europe fuelling the anti-immigrant and Islamophobic hysteria – one of the main reasons for BREXIT and the triumph of Trump.

I cite Pilger as an example of a journalist who has the courage to tell the truth. He quotes the Soviet dissident Yevtushenko: "When the truth is replaced by silence, the silence is a lie." A large part of the Western media is silenced by the Establishment.

Trump and the revolt against the establishment

We are back to the question: would Trump make a difference? To be frank, I don't know. The odds are heavily against him.

The odds were against Bernie Sanders too. He contested Hillary Clinton, but later he gave in to her. He had an enormous following amongst the younger generation - angry, frustrated, suffering from financial crisis, and rising inequality. The Gini coefficient is a measure of inequality in which 0 is perfect equality and 100 is perfect inequality, or one person owning all the wealth. According to one estimate, the Gini coefficient of the USA is 80.56. It is one of the most unequal countries in the world. [28]

So why did Sanders step down? He probably realised that it was futile to challenge the Establishment that backed Clinton. With all the support he had among the people, only 29% of primary voters supported him compared 47% for Clinton.

THE TRUMP PHENOMENON & THE EMERGENCE OF A NEW WORLD ORDER

So what is the difference between Sanders and Trump? One important difference is that, unlike Sanders, Trump has his own resources. He did not have to depend on the Republican Party either politically or financially. Trump managed to become US president by tapping into the anti-establishment anger of a declining middle class – where Sanders failed.

How far would Trump be able to challenge the Establishment and the Deep State? This remains to be seen. In an interesting development, Sanders said that he would be happy to work with Trump provided he saved the social safety nets. He would work with Trump on trade and keeping American companies from moving jobs abroad. "Financial deregulation, brought about during the Clinton administration", Sanders said, "which allowed commercial banks and investment banks and large insurance companies to merge, created the pathway forward to the collapse of 2008."[29] Here is Sanders distancing himself, again, from Clinton.

By way of conclusion

1.	The Deep State, the "state within the state" is a reality. It is "the Establishment" that backed Clinton against Trump, but failed. Trump was able to feed on the anger of the people disillusioned with the Establishment.

2.	One reason Trump succeeded where Sanders failed was his financial independence.

3.	That does not ensure that Trump will deliver on his promises. The Establishment will try and direct him back to its own agenda. The media still remains part of the Establishment, though it seems it may kowtow to Trump opportunistically.

4.	Bernie Sanders may try and "radicalise" the Democratic Party, just as Trump may try to "reform" the Republicans. Whether they succeed or not remains to be seen. But it is interesting that Sanders is prepared to work with Trump on certain issues.

5.	Finally, those of us who are in the global South can take a leaf out of Sanders' book – seize the space provided by the change in the US presidency.

PART FIVE

THE GLOBAL MILITARY-SECURITY DIMENSION

Introduction

Trump has challenged the Europeans on the issue of contributions to NATO, provoking speculation that NATO's future might be at stake. From NATO's Secretariat the reaction was strong. Secretary General Jens Stoltenberg warned Trump that the West is facing its "greatest challenge to security in a generation", and America's "going alone is not an option".[30]

NATO's former Deputy Supreme Allied Commander in Europe, General Sir Richard Shirreff's recent book, *War with Russia*, was described by the *Sunday Times* as a "Top Ten Bestseller". It gives a chilling account of how Russia has become increasingly militaristic, embroiling itself in conflicts in Ukraine and Syria. Sir Richard (born in Kenya) criticised British Government's paltry spending on defence.

Here is the power of the military. But the military is only part of a bigger complex.

The Military-Industrial-Financial Complex

The American President and a military man, General Dwight D. Eisenhower, in his Farewell Address on January 17, 1961, alerted the Americans to guard against the influence of the *military-industrial complex*. He knew how the MIC marshalled political support for increased military spending in the interest of their profits.

In his *U.S. Imperialism And America's War Machine: A Destructive Apparatus*, (2013) William C. Lewis argued that Corporate Imperial Militarism controls U.S. society and wages destructive occupations abroad to serve the capitalist interest in wars - making and selling arms to kill people for profit.[32]

To the Military Industrial Complex must be added the *Banking-Financial dimension*.

At the beginning of World War I, President Woodrow Wilson had initially adopted a policy of neutrality. But Morgan Bank, which funded over 75 percent of the financing for the allied forces during the War, pushed Wilson out of neutrality sooner than he might have gone.[33]

In her *All the Presidents' Bankers: The Hidden Alliances that Drive American Power*, Nomi Prins, drawing on original presidential archival documents, shows the intimate link between the White House (the State) and Wall Street (Finance Capital). Prins should know. She had worked as managing director

at Goldman Sachs, as a Lehman Brothers strategist, and as a Chase Manhattan Bank analyst. Then she left the world of finance. "I was probably soul-searching a while before I left ... when I got to Goldman Sachs I realized that the nature of how business was done was not something I wanted to be involved with".[34] The triumvirate – *Industry, the military, and finance capital* - are behind wars and the pervasive culture of militarism in the build-up of the Anglo-Saxon and European Empire. To take one recent example, Britain sold £3.3 billion of arms to Saudi Arabia in the first year of Saudi bombardment of Yemen. In a November, 2016 debate in the British Parliament, the leader of the Opposition, Jeremy Corbyn, called on the Prime Minister to halt those sales because of the "humanitarian devastation" caused by a Saudi-led coalition waging war against rebels in Yemen. In her defence, Theresa May said Britain must go on selling these arms to "keep people on the streets of Britain safe".[35]

The state in Britain and the arms industry go hand in hand. Theresa May should know that as more people flow out of the Middle East because of the wars the military-industrial-financial complex promotes, the less safety there is for the "streets of Britain".

Europe, Vassal of USA

Paul Craig Roberts is an American economist, journalist, and now a well-known blogger. He was the US Assistant Secretary of State under President Reagan in 1981. He is critical of mainstream politicians, including Bush and Obama, especially in their handling of the "War on Terror", which he views as threatening constitutional civil liberties and right to privacy of ordinary Americans.

In his "America's Conquest of Western Europe: Is Europe Doomed By Vassalage To Washington?" he shows how the Second World War ended in Europe being conquered not by Germany but by the USA. The US used not the military but the financial muscle, the mighty US Dollar. The US Establishment encouraged the integration of Europe into the EU. The EU created its own currency. Smaller countries such as Greece, Portugal, Latvia, and Ireland who can no longer create their own money have been looted by the private banks from whom they borrow to finance their debts.

THE TRUMP PHENOMENON & THE EMERGENCE OF A NEW WORLD ORDER

Why, Craig asks, do these governments, despite expressed wishes of the people (like in Greece) continue to remain in the European Union? His answer is: "… that Washington would have it no other way. The European founders of the EU are mythical creatures. Washington used politicians that Washington controlled to create the EU". These "pseudo-governments" are obliged to privatise public assets, run down social welfare, and cut retirement pensions in order to pay their debts to German banks. It is no wonder that during Obama's last farewell tour of Europe, he described Chancellor Merkel as "my closest international partner these past eight years."[36] He ended his tour by offering advice to Trump: "Stand up to Russia".[37]

Trump's imperial legacy from Monroe Doctrine to today

Before we come to assess Trump's foreign policy, it is important to provide a brief historical context of where the US comes from and where it is going.

In 1783 the 13 American colonies declared independence from England after a bitter war that lasted eight years. Alexander Hamilton writing in the "Federalist Papers" was already talking about the emergent America as a world power – particularly in relation to the western hemisphere, principally in North America. This was later extended to Latin America in 1823 under the Monroe Doctrine, which declared that any effort by Europe to take control of North or South America would be viewed as "the manifestation of an unfriendly disposition toward the United States." At the time the Spanish and Portuguese Empires were collapsing, and their colonies were vying for independence.

In his "The Monroe Doctrine: Empire and Nation in 19th-Century America" (2011) Jay Sexton shows how the doctrine evolved over time. At the time of its formulation, there was fear not only of European threat to the US but also of the USA breaking apart.

What followed then was the expansion of the US Empire in Latin America and the Pacific. It is a chequered history where Europe retained hold over some countries in the region… to this day. Here are some highlights of Euro-American imperial conquests before the First World War.

- In 1842, the Monroe Doctrine was applied to Hawaii, Britain was warned to keep out, and the US annexed Hawaii.

- In 1838-50 Argentina was blockaded by the French and, later, the British. No action was taken by the US.

- In early 1843, England reasserted its sovereignty over the Falkland Islands. No action was taken by the US.

- In 1862, taking advantage of the American Civil War (1862-1867), the French invaded and conquered Mexico. The US denounced it as a violation of the Monroe Doctrine, and in 1865, it stationed a large army on the Mexican border, and encouraged a revolution against France's stooge, Maximilian, who was executed by the Mexican nationalists. France pulled out, and Mexico became a virtual colony of the US – to this day.

- In 1862, The British turned Belize into a crown colony and renamed it British Honduras. The US took no action.

- In 1898, the US intervened in support of Cuba during its war for independence from Spain. Under the terms of the peace treaty from which Cuba was excluded, Spain ceded Puerto Rico, the Philippines, and Guam to the US in exchange for $20 million. Cuba came under US control and remained so until it was granted formal independence in 1902.

- In 1901 Theodore Roosevelt became US's 26th President. By this time the US was well past the civil war and imperialism was in full force. The Americans believed that they have a "manifest destiny" to redeem the world from the evils of European imperialism and spread "the special virtues of the American people and their institutions".[38] In 1904 Roosevelt extended the Monroe Doctrine (called the "*Roosevelt Corollary*"), asserting the right of the US to intervene in Latin America in cases of "flagrant and chronic wrongdoing" by a Latin American Nation. Under his "speak low and carry a big stick" foreign policy, Roosevelt proceeded to virtually colonise any Latin American nation that failed to pay their debts to European and US banks and business interests.

Let us fast track to more recent times. There have been a series of US interventions in Latin America during the cold war period and in recent times to fight revolutionary movements and/or to carry out "regime changes" in Argentina, Bolivia, Chile, Dominical Republic, El Salvador, Haiti, Grenada, Honduras, Mexico, Nicaragua, Panama, Puerto Rico and Venezuela.[38]

Here are a few instances of these:

- In 1954, Secretary of State John Foster Dulles invoked the Monroe Doctrine at the 10th Pan-American Conference in Caracas (Venezuela), denouncing the intervention of Soviet Communism in Guatemala.

- After the Cuban Revolution (1953–1959) when Fidel Castro established ties with the Soviet Union, the US invoked the Monroe Doctrine to prevent the spread of Soviet-backed Communism in Latin America.

- In 2009, Secretary of State Clinton aided the military coup in Honduras against democratically elected president Manuel Zelaya.[40]

The above account can be multiplied several times over if we were to include the other regions of the Global South – the Middle East (including Iran), Asia, and Africa. It is this imperial legacy – the "Imperial Burden" - that Trump is expected to carry.

Trump's foreign policy challenges

Would Trump succeed in carrying the imperial burden? It is too early to say, but it will, undoubtedly, be a compromise between what he and his inner circle of policy advisers intend to do, and what the military-industrial-financial Establishment complex wants him to do.

Let us look at some specific issues.

- His first hurdle would be the massive anti-Russian hoopla mounted by the US, the UK and the European Union.[41]

- Overall, Trump is for peace and diplomatic resolution of international conflicts. This has unleashed reactions bordering on hysteria. Jonathan Powell, writing for the *Guardian*, said, "The US is dangerously exposed by an isolationist Trump".[42] Owen Jones, also writing for the *Guardian*, said, "Our crisis is existential … Trump's victory is one of the biggest calamities to befall the west". [43]

- Trump had said during the election campaign that he would try to renegotiate the nuclear deal agreement with Iran, and increase US sanctions against Iran. He has since then retracted a bit, but the pressure from some of his inner circles and from Israel may cause some hurdles for him.

- On the Israel–Palestine conflict, Trump has given assurances to Benjamin Netanyahu. At the same time, however, he has said that he would "love to be the one" to make peace between the two.

- Trump is likely to take a tougher stand on Cuba than Obama, and possibly take a more interventionist position in relation to the rest of Latin America.

On mega-trade agreements - such as the TPP and the TIPP – Trump had said during the electoral campaign trail that he would get rid of them. He did with the TPP; he well might do it with the TIPP. But, and this is important, we should understand that these are only partly trade deals. Essentially, they are part of the US strategy to isolate Russia (in the case of TTIP) and China (under TPP). China and Russia are seen as military threats. Trump is a "nationalist", (as defined earlier), and has taken the anti-TPP-TTIP position, as he has in relation to the NATO. But this is not the last on these mega-regional trade deals because they have a bigger military-security importance than economic.

Some Concluding Remarks

The years 2017 to 2020 are likely to shatter many shibboleths of the past years. The stage has already been set by events like the Brexit, Trump's presidency, the anti-Russian hysteria among the Euro-American Establishment, the rise of the populist right in much of Europe, and above all, the deepening financial and global systemic crisis.

We still have to see the end of the gruesome wars in the Middle East, and their military-security consequences. The geopolitics of the East Asia region are shifting the balance of forces in favour of China. We need to watch how the US will react to this unfolding scenario.

There will be continuing struggles to keep Europe intact and to hold on to the North Atlantic Treaty Organisation (NATO). Already NATO is under severe strain - Europe led by Germany and France might try to create a European Security organisation, but I think it will fail; and in time to come the European Union will fragment.

An accidental nuclear exchange in some of the hotspots of the globe cannot be ruled out.

PART SIX

WHAT IS FASCISM IN OUR TIMES?

There is much talk these days, especially in the Western media, about "fascism". The word is thrown around with total abandon to describe any political figure with whom one is in disagreement. Sometimes, "fascism" is twinned with "populism" so that those that are described as "fascists" - for example Trump in America and Le Pen in France - are also called "populists".

The West is caught up in a historical trap from which its people (including the intelligentsia) are unable to escape.[44] History has entrapped them. The result is that they have no longer much to offer in order for us to understand what fascism really means today.

Those who do not recognise the turning points of history cannot even raise the right questions, let alone provide answers to some the glaring challenges we now face.

Classical Fascism

In his essay, "The Essence of Fascism" (1935), Karl Polanyi wrote: "Victorious Fascism is not only the downfall of the Socialist Movement; it is the end of Christianity in all but its most debased forms. The common attack of German Fascism on both the organisations of the working-class movement and the Churches is not a mere coincidence. It is a symbolic expression of that hidden philosophical essence of Fascism which makes it the common enemy of Socialism and Christianity alike."[45]

In another essay Polanyi wrote:" Fascism is born from the incompatibility between democracy and capitalism in a fully developed industrial society. Either capitalism or democracy must therefore disappear. Fascism constitutes the solution to this deadlock by allowing capitalism to persist."[46]

Polanyi was right about the incompatibility between capitalism and democracy. Eighty years later, on July 22 2015, the British Foreign Secretary, Philip Hammond, told members of the British Parliament that democracy was "cumbersome" for the pursuit of foreign military objectives. He said democracy puts Western governments at a disadvantage in confronting Russia and other threats: "We as a nation and as part of an alliance in NATO must think about how we deal with the challenge of our relatively cumbersome decision-making processes."[47] (https://www.rt.com/uk/310448-cumbersome-democracy-russia-isis/)

Fascism of the Hegemonic/Imperialist Powers

In his "The Return of Fascism in Contemporary Capitalism", Samir Amin explains how the hegemonic capitalist/imperialist powers embodied fascism in their relations with the rest of the world, and how its roots go back to Nazism. [48]

> Nazism is the model of this type of fascism. Germany became a major industrial power beginning in the 1870s and a competitor of the hegemonic powers of the era (Great Britain and, secondarily, France) and of the country that aspired to become hegemonic (the United States). … Japanese fascism belongs to the same category. Since 1895, modern capitalist Japan aspired to impose its domination over all of East Asia…. Nazi Germany made an alliance with imperial/fascist Japan.

I'll quote Samir Amin at some length for the readers to understand the origins and essence of contemporary fascism that is obfuscated by loose use of the term "fascism" by the political elite and popular media in the West to which I referred earlier. Says Amin:

> The right in European parliaments between the two world wars was always complaisant about fascism and even about the more repugnant Nazism. Churchill himself, regardless of his extreme "Britishness", never hid his sympathy for Mussolini. … With all the cynicism characteristic of the U.S. establishment, Truman openly avowed what others thought quietly: allow the war to wear out its protagonists - Germany, Soviet Russia, and the defeated Europeans - and intervene as late as possible to reap the benefits…. No hesitation was shown in the rehabilitation of Salazar and Franco in 1945. Furthermore, connivance with European fascism was a constant in the policy of the Catholic Church. It would not strain credibility to describe Pius XII as a collaborator with Mussolini and Hitler. … Hitler's anti-Semitism itself aroused opprobrium only much later, when it reached the ultimate stage of its murderous insanity.

Amin, then, explains how and why the socialist and social-democratic parties of Western and Central Europe enabled fascism to return in full force today.

In West Germany, in the name of "reconciliation," the local government and its patrons (the United States, and secondarily Great Britain and France) left in place nearly all those who had committed war crimes and crimes against humanity.... [It was] the support of the socialist and social-democratic parties of Western and Central Europe for the anti-communist campaigns undertaken by the conservative right [that] shares responsibility for the later return of fascism.

Corporate Fascism

Political philosopher, Sheldon Wolin, described the emerging form of government of the United States as "illiberal democracy". He used the term "inverted totalitarianism" to describe the system of democracy in the US. He

goes on to show that the "liberal church", like the rest of the "liberal establishment", looked the other way while the poor and working people, especially those of colour, were ruthlessly disempowered and impoverished.

The term "inverted totalitarianism" was picked up by, among others, Chris Hedges and Joe Sacco. In *Days of Destruction, Days of Revolt* they describe how corporations have corrupted and subverted democracy, and how people are manipulated into surrendering their liberties and their participation in government through commodification of natural and human resources in a deeply ingrained consumerist culture.

Roger Moody in his *Rocks and Hard Places: The Globalisation of Mining* argues that both communities and fragile ecosystems are unable to cope with bigger and bigger mining ventures. As grades of ore decline, and community opposition mounts, mega mining corporations are taking over more and more Greenfield sites in the global South.[49]

We know it from our own experience in Africa how global corporations have been exploiting African nations for their minerals – oil, iron ore, aluminium, diamond, uranium, gold, zinc, copper and cobalt – to mention only the obvious ones.

The Southern and Eastern African Trade Information and Negotiations Institute (SEATINI) – which I founded in 1997 – has been having running battles in the World Trade Organisation (WTO) and with the European Union (EU) encouraging African governments to resist the pressures from the Western corporations to open up their countries to exploitation. We have had some successes, but the corporations, backed by their states and institutions of global economic governance are simply too powerful. To describe them as "fascist" would be quite appropriate.

These fascist methods that can only be described as acts of "war" are used not just against the nations of the South, but also against the peoples of First Nations. Take the case of the hotly contested Dakota Access Pipeline (DAPL) in the United States. The DAPL is a 1,172-mile-long underground oil pipeline under construction by a number of corporations – including Dakota Access, a part subsidiary of Energy Transfer Partners. The pipeline is guarded by the G4S (a leading global integrated security company) that uses psychological warfare tactics - fascist methods - to guard the pipeline against the people.[50] The Standing Rock and Cheyenne River Sioux tribes (among others) have opposed the DAPL arguing that the pipeline threatens their "way of life, their water, people, and land.[51]

In my earlier blogs, I have described how Euro-American Imperial Militarism serves corporate interests through waging wars and encouraging the manufacturing of armaments that eradicate human beings for profit.Global corporations like Cargill and Union Carbide and especially manufacturers of weapons of war; the revolving doors between them and state bureaucracies in the imperial states; the strategic hold these states have over institutions of global governance such as the IMF, the World Banks and the WTO; and the looting of the scientific knowledge of the communities in the South which have developed this knowledge over thousands of years - all these constitute theft and corruption at the highest levels.

Financial Fascism

The whole system of corporate fascism is supported by a complex web of banking and financial institutions. I have written on this subject, so I will not go into this again. But take the case of Mark Johnson, HSBC's global head of foreign exchange trading, who was charged of fraud in the US for his alleged role in using inside information to profit from a major currency deal. Strange though it may sound, but I must say this in his defence that he is not personally accountable for the fraud; the whole banking system is a fraud that enjoys impunity. Indeed, the global financial superstructure fits well with Sheldon Wolin's concept of "inverted totalitarianism".

Some Conclusions

1. Fascism is a systemic, structural, phenomenon, not personal. Individuals in state power who "administer" the system are often stigmatised as "fascist". The person becomes the most visible carrier of the fascist project.

2. It follows that those in state power in the African neo-colonies administer the fascist system on behalf of corporate and financial fascism. Of course, some are more ruthless than others. They are dictators or militarists, and the continent is full of them. Others, like Nyerere, are democratic and anti-imperialist, but the corporate power is too strong for them to turn around a deeply embedded fascistic coloniality of the state and the economy.

3. The Euro-American Imperial Militarism serves corporate interests through waging wars against not only the people of the Global South but also their own people, especially the workers, the people of First Nations, and the people of colour.

4. This series of blogs began on November 15, 2016 with my reflections on the US elections. Part 1 was on "Trump and Trumpism" where I will argue that Trump is an anti-Establishment capitalist. From an African perspective, we can work with him if he defies the WTO; rejects mega-regional Trade and Investment treaties like the TPP and the TTIP;

scraps AGOA; and talks with Russia, China and Iran for peaceful resolution of conflicts.

5.   In Part 7 - "The Politics of Resistance and Solidarity"- I argue that the Western world is in turmoil. We do not know how this will evolve. But if it breaks down the European Union, dismantles NATO, weakens the Empire's financial control over the global South, and opens a space for a new moral and political order to emerge, then it is an opportunity we must seize.

6.   This said, I must warn that the newest phase of Imperial Fascism is all the more dangerous, and aggressive, because the Western Empire is facing its crisis point, its denouement.

7.   Every crisis, however, is also an opportunity. That is so provided we understand the underlying forces:

Trump himself may be a passing phenomenon. But he is today's reality. He will be the President of the wealthiest and militarily the most powerful country in the world with a finger on the nuclear trigger. He can decide the fate of millions inside and outside his country. So let us take stock where we from the South fit into this emerging reality against the background of a collapsing Empire and an emergent new world with all its perils and promises. The past is not dead ground, and to traverse it is not a sterile exercise. The challenges lie here and now.

PART SEVEN

POLITICS OF RESISTANCE AND SOLIDARITY

The Civilizational Shift

Let us put the Trump phenomenon in a wider context – that of a civilizational shift – a slow, painful demise of the Western Empire. In contrast to Francis Fukuyama's "End of History" and Huntington's "The Clash of Civilizations", I prefer to talk about "The Civilizational Shift".[52] In my book *Trade is War*,[53] I argued that no civilization, however defined[54], lasts forever. Contrary to what most people think (or believe) the so-called Western or capitalist civilization is not everlasting. This civilization's callous exploitation of human labour and nature is finally coming to an end. It may take yet another century, but that is not really too long to wait. Civilizations previous to capitalism (such as the Aztec, Egyptian, Chinese, Indian and Persian) lasted much longer.

Trump himself may be a passing phenomenon. But he is today's reality. He is the president of the wealthiest and militarily the most powerful country in the world with a finger on the nuclear trigger. He can decide the fate of millions inside and outside his country.

So let us take stock where we from the South fit into this emerging reality against the background of a collapsing Empire and an emergent new world with all its perils and promises. The past is not dead ground, and to traverse it is not a sterile exercise. The challenges lie here and now.

The Communist Manifesto is dead

Karl Marx thought that the international proletariat would be capitalism's nemesis. It might still be; we do not know.

Bound by his own time and space, Marx's perspective was still essentially Eurocentric, and hence his memorable phrase: "A spectre is haunting Europe — the spectre of communism". In our own time, it is now the spectre of the oppressed nations of the world (most significantly, the nationalism of the countries of the South) that is "haunting Europe" … and America.

And here is where we might take a leaf from Sanders' book when referring to Trump's victory in the US elections. Sanders said he is prepared to work with Trump provided Trump protects matters of social security. On our part in the South, I suggest we work with Trump provided he respects our nationalism and our sovereignty. We resist him if he tries, like Obama, to continue with the US policy of "regime change" in the global South.

In Part 3 I had described Trump as an "economic nationalist". The Western "left-liberal" political and intellectual forces find it odd that Trump is a "nationalist". How can this be? Surely, they might say, Trump is living out of his time; surely, there is no room for nationalism in our times.

We must tell our friends in the North with whom we wish to work in solidarity towards a peaceful and just world, that Trump is not an oddity in our times. Nationalism is not out of fashion. *As long as the world is cut up into nation-states there will be be nationalism.* In fact, nationalism has returned to Europe and the Americas with a vengeance. The campaign calling for the independence of California from the United Sates has been calling for "Calexit", and has opened an "embassy" in Moscow. [55]

Aggressive and defensive nationalisms

We must distinguish between two very different species of nationalisms – one offensive and the other defensive. A bit of history is a good guide. The first kind of nationalism – the aggressive and fascist - was put in place by Mussolini when he became Italy's Prime Minister in 1922. He appealed to the popular sense of Italy's imperial past and promoted its restoration in the Mediterranean Sea and Africa. He built closer relations with Germany, especially after Hitler became its Chancellor in January 1933. In October 1935, with a 100,000 strong army Mussolini invaded the ancient land of Abyssinia (now Ethiopia). In Germany Hitler declared war on two fronts – internally against the Jews; and externally against Europe as a prelude to conquer the world for a "pure" Aryan race.

Then there is the "defensive nationalism". The anti-colonial struggle for liberation from the European Empire was defensive. The continuing struggle of the Global South (Asia, Africa, Latin America and the Caribbean) from the American-European-Japanese imperialism is defensive nationalism.

This does not contradict our effort at regional integration – for example, the East African Community. Unlike the European Union, which is an aggressive project, the EAC is a defensive project.

Aggressive nationalism in our times and Trump's challenge

Aggressive nationalism is imperialist. Its most virulent organisational expression is the North Atlantic Treaty Organisation (NATO). _NATO is the main source of global insecurity today._ Our "left-liberal" solidarity friends in the North might contest this, and argue that the "terrorists" (especially Islamic terrorists) are the main source of insecurity. In a curious way this is true. But they must know that the "terrorists" are a product of Western wars in the Middle East and Africa. These wars in Iraq, Afghanistan, Libya, Syria, Yemen, Mali, Somalia – to name a few - have only added fuel to terrorist fire.

Trump has said that NATO is obsolete, and he wants to talk with Putin; that he will renegotiate the Iran nuclear deal; he will stand by Israel against the Palestinians; he will challenge China's hegemony in trade, and by extension, possibly in the area of the military in East Asia; and so on. It is a mixed bag. What he will actually do remains to be seen. Nonetheless, it is correct to assume that NATO will not disappear overnight, and the Empire will not withdraw its claws from its imperialist outreach the world over. Nonetheless, if Trump does act on his ideas to question NATO and to talk with Russia (on matters related to Europe and the Middle East), then we in the South should cooperate with him.

THE TRUMP PHENOMENON & THE EMERGENCE OF A NEW WORLD ORDER

Trump is "defensive" when it comes to protecting the American economy and employment from what he regards as "invasion" by cheap products from the South, mainly China, and illegal immigrants, mainly from border countries like Mexico. Of course, we know that the issues of unemployment and lack of competitiveness in the global market are complex matters. They are as much related to the impact of technology on production (what Marx called the changing "organic composition of capital"[56]), as of "cheap imports" from China, and immigrants from Mexico.

But Trump may well take some "defensive" or "protectionist" measures to defend America's economy. There are two aspects of these measures that might be of interest to us in the South. One is his opposition to the World Trade Organization (WTO), and the second his opposition to the mega-regional trade and investment agreements that we discussed in an earlier piece.

Trump appears to defy the mainstream neoclassical ideology that "free trade" is good for all. He is definitely for protection. During his campaigns he even threatened to pull the US out of the WTO if it blocks his efforts to impose penalties on companies that move American production offshore. Again, this is a complex issue. But Trump is right; "free trade" is not good for all. It has been disastrous for Africa and most of the weaker countries of the South. If Trump becomes "protectionist", this would add weight to the efforts of the countries in the global South to put barriers against imports that threaten value-added production at home. I have argued in my book *Trade is War* that the WTO is a war machine wielded by the West against the global South.

Defensive nationalism in our times and the National Question

On the defensive kind of nationalism, the efforts by the peoples of the countries of the South – from Cuba to Congo to China – to try and consolidate their independence from Western-backed aggressions will continue. These countries are still battling with their "National Question", a historically defined incomplete liberation from imperialism; a strategic issue that is largely absent from the vocabulary of our Western "solidarity" friends.[57]

But a more interesting current phenomenon is the emergence of "defensive nationalism" within Europe too. For them it is not a part of the "National Question" – as defined above. But it is still part of the efforts to protect their national identities against encroachments by bigger powers. Greece has become an emblematic case, its effort to protect its national sovereignty crushed by the triumvirate of the European Commission, the European Central Bank and the IMF.

But there are other cases – Scotland and possibly Ireland in the United Kingdom; the Walloons in Belgium; the Basque in France; and Catalonia in Spain. Interestingly, a wave of " nationalism" has hit even major countries like England, France and Italy where people are voting in vast numbers to pull out of what they see as the domination of the unelected bureaucrats in the European Commission. The victory of François Fillon in the French Republican presidential primary on 27 November 2016, and in Italy, the popular rejection (by nearly 60%) of Prime Minister Matteo Renzi's attempt to reform the Constitution on 4 December 2016 referendum … are interesting signs on the horizon of what might be a new kind of Europe in months and years to come.

Globalisation versus Internationalism

The Western "left-liberals" have now joined forces with their ruling classes in defence of "globalisation". In their dictionary "globalisation" is uncritically identified with "internationalism". For us in the South, "globalisation" is simply a sanitised version of "imperialism". I have all these terms into inverted commas, because we assume, when we use these, that we are all agreed on their definitions. Words matter. They arise at a particular time in history and specific contexts. That's why Lenin defined "imperialism" as the "highest stage of capitalism" in his time, and Nkrumah defined it as "neo-colonialism" in our time. The reality remains – that of capitalist-imperialist continued predation of the colonies and neo-colonies.

Some thoughts for the future: politics of solidarity

The future we talk about is the foreseeable future – say the next 20 years, a generation.

Within the next 20-25 years, we'll witness further signs of the decline of Western civilization; there is a palpable civilizational shift. As the geopolitical balance of forces shift from the West to the ancient civilizations of the past, we cannot be sure if the new civilizations will necessarily be any better.

The last century's wars of national liberation brought a degree of political freedom to the two-thirds humanity in the global South encaged in capitalist-imperialist slavery. But the "National Question" remains a challenge for most of them.

The era of "socialism" has been short lived. But we have learnt valuable lessons from the successes and failures of socialism in the Soviet Union, China, Vietnam, and countries in Africa and Latin America. Cuba under Fidel Castro has been an outstanding example of how to sustain a system of social justice and social welfare (education, health, housing, etc.) against the background of 50 years of relentless sanctions by the biggest power on earth literally 50 miles away.

The Western world is in turmoil. Karl Polanyi had said that there is a symbiotic link between global capital and state power reproduced as "Globalised Fascism". That is what we are living through. We do not know how the wave of "rightist" populism that has engulfed Europe and American will evolve. But if it breaks down the European Union, dismantles NATO, weakens the Empire's financial control over the global South, and opens a space for a new moral and political order to emerge, then it is an opportunity we must seize.

The "we" is difficult to define. To call ourselves "the left" is to live in the past. The "left" in Europe is very different from the "left" in Africa. For sure, there are common principles of social justice we share. There are common battles we fight – for example, for a system fair trade; for free exchange of knowledge appropriated by global corporations as their "intellectual property" rights; and for a revolution in the way we relate to the environment and the other livings species – primates, wildlife and forests.

It is in this context that we who call ourselves the "left" must work out new principles of solidarity based on mutual respect, working together as equals and without exploitation, to advance shared values.

For their part, the "left" in Africa must help our leaders to develop self-reliant economies and governance systems. Africa must end its shameful dependence on the so-called "development aid". In a new world, Africa must use its own resources, knowledge and ingenuity, and produce its own food, fishing nets, and democratic systems of governance. This is happening, but more needs to be done.

POSTSCRIPT

A WHIRLWIND OF CHANGE

Who is Trump?

President Trump is highly unconventional and in some odd ways, an innovative figure in American history. He not only defeated all his 16 Republican rivals in the primaries, but - without any real experience in government – he went on to challenge not only the Democratic but also his own Party. And he won. He is really neither a Republican nor a Democrat.

In one of the pieces in this booklet, I explain why. It is partly because of his skills, but also because times have changed within America and globally. Some psychoanalysts have described him as an "emotions candidate". He dominated his audience – many of them young, mostly white - who responded to his evocation of national pride and collective spirit. He had few concrete policy prescriptions to offer. He is a capitalist, albeit a self-made capitalist; but he is not part of the Establishment. Trump's campaign trail had so much venom against the immigrants, the Muslims, and other "out-groups" and ethnic minorities that it grossly violated the left- liberal moral zeitgeist - anti-racist, pro-immigrant, pro-LGBT, internationalist, and so on. But he is a "nationalist"; his campaigning slogan was: "Make America Great Again!"

Offensive versus defensive nationalism

For reasons of clarity, I have also argued in one of my pieces, that Trump and we from Africa (and the global South) represent two polarized strands of nationalism. He comes from an American imperial past - representing aggressive nationalism. I am from Africa - ours is defensive nationalism. It is aimed at completing the struggle for national independence from imperial globalised fascism. It is an important distinction - one that is largely ignored not only by the hugely ignorant Western media but also by the "liberal-left" Western intelligentsia, political elite, and the academia. They have a blind spot that obliterates the National Question from their vision.

In one of the pieces – "Imperialism, Nationalism and the National Question" - I go to great lengths to clarify the significance of the National Question for us. Imperialism is an existential reality in our times. Western denial of it arises out of what I call the Intransigent Imperialism Rejection Syndrome (IIRS). Today imperialism exists in its sanitised version - it is called "Free Trade Globalisation". There is a lot of hullabaloo about nationalism and fascism in the West, but there is no recognition that their entire system is fascist.

Western "economic nationalism" is an imperial fascist project

All aggressive nationalism turns fascist. Trump and people like Le Pen in France are called "nationalist" and "fascist". I have a problem with this. As I understand it, fascism is a systemic, structural, phenomenon, not personal. This is important. A leader of a "democratic" country might be elected by the people "democratically", but if the country is imperialist, then the leader is heading a fascist state. *The USA is a fascist state.* Obama might have been elected democratically, but his foreign policy was fascist. US will spend $1 trillion over next 30 years - i.e. $1,000,000,000,000 (yes, 12 zeros) - to "modernise" its weapons of mass destruction. It was proposed by Obama/Clinton. Trump has inherited an imperial fascist state. In UK, Prime Minister Teresa May has defended selling military hardware to Saudi Arabia that has devastated the population of Yemen. She is presiding over an imperial fascist state.

In one of the pieces I have taken the help of Karl Polanyi to explain this to Western audiences. He described the link between global capital and state power as "Globalised Fascism". He defined capitalism's complete takeover of the political sphere as the "fascist project". Only with complete control of the political sphere, he said, will capitalism do away with limits imposed for instance by labor and environmental protection laws.

I take Polanyi's argument and take it one step further. Let's not be mistaken about it: the aim (consciously or unconsciously) of all those supporting the imperialist trade agreements, such as the TTIP (the Transatlantic Trade & Investments Partnership) is to transform the global economy into a single market where democracy and elected governments will have no meaning anymore. Instead, an elite corporate oligarchy will become the real masters of the world.

The emperor has no clothes

In an interesting interview titled "Democracy Collaborative", the American Marxist political economist, Michael Hudson, says: "What's new is that Trump said the emperor has no clothes".[58]

Let me give a fuller quote from Hudson - it says it all:

> When Hillary tried to convince people they were better off, Trump simply said, "Let's look at reality: You're worse off." ... Trump said NATO's obsolete. There's no reason for us to maintain it—Russia's not going to invade Europe. Why should they invade? There's no way any European country is going to militarily invade another. The new mode of warfare isn't military anymore, it's financial. ... Trump realized that as a real estate developer, he'd been fighting banks all his life. ... So the neocons are out to get him. They're saying it is treason to want peace instead of war. We need an enemy sufficient enough to justify giving all the surplus to the upper 5% and spending it on the military. If you don't advocate doing that, you're a traitor – to their fortunes. So they're out to get rid of him.

Looking to the future

No civilization, however defined, lasts forever. We are witnessing a civilizational shift - a slow, painful demise of the Western Empire. This cannot be understood unless you have a long civilizational worldview. Civilizations such as - among others - Egyptian, Chinese, Indian, Persian, Greek, Islamic, Russian, and the Aztec - have existed for hundreds - in some cases for thousands - of years before the rise of the western imperial civilization barely 500 years old. "Our" current civilization was founded on the slave trade (mainly from Africa), and the rise of capitalism. This - the Euro-American Civilization - is collapsing even as we read these lines, challenged in our times by the rise of China and Russia and the resistance by the peoples of the Islamic nations.

Because of institutionalized racism, this part of history is generally lost to the West. Barring the more enlightened individuals, people in the West are socio-psychologically tuned to a certain hubris about the 'higher' quality of Western civilization as opposed to the 'lower' civilizations of Africa and the Orient. There is a commonly held perception that the life of an ordinary African, Afghan, Palestinian or Muslim is worth nothing compared to the life or rights of an ordinary "white" person. This hubris poisons ordinary relations between

THE TRUMP PHENOMENON & THE EMERGENCE OF A NEW WORLD ORDER

the West and the Rest. This is the stark - and sad - reality of the contemporary postcolonial world.

Of course we cannot go back to the past.

I recommend to readers a book that I recently reviewed.[59] Its 19 African writers cover an extensive ground, but there is a common thread that runs through their essays. Since the rise of the nation-state in mid-16th Century Europe, nationalism, they say, has been a contested site. It expresses itself in many forms - its worst expressions being racism, colonialism and fascism.

At the global level, they say, the National Question is still an unresolved national project. Several of them addressed the important subject of coloniality, neo-coloniality and de-coloniality. Whilst colonialism was a historical phase, coloniality is an embedded structure. It manifests itself primarily at the economic level, but some of its worst manifestations are rooted in the existing power structures and their ideological expressions. One of the editors puts it well: "The final tenet is control of subjectivity and knowledge involving epistemic colonisation." I have lectured up and down many universities in Europe and America, and I can provide evidence of "epistemic colonisation" even among African academics, as well as Western.

So where do we move from here?

First we need to "decolonize" our minds. We need to challenge the economic orthodoxy, and work on development alternatives that take into account the fact that all countries - without exception - are economic nationalists, including those that swear by the ideology of "free market globalisation". Africa must "decouple" from fascist globalisation through active resistance against, for example, the dictates of the World Trade Organisation and the European Union's imposed so-called "Economic Partnership Agreements".

Economic nationalism does not preclude regionalism - nations getting together to integrate regionally. In fact, for Africa to get rid of the yoke of European and American imperialism it is imperative that they integrate at a continental level, though starting, at first, at regional level as prescribed by, for example, the Lagos Plan of Action that the African Union agreed to in April 1980 - a plan that has been systematically subverted by the World Bank, acting for the Empire.

Most importantly, we all – not just Africans but the whole world - should listen to Martin Luther King, who embraced Gandhi's nonviolent Satyagraha legacy. Four days before he was cruelly murdered, he said: "It is no longer a choice, my friends, between violence and nonviolence. It is either nonviolence or nonexistence".

@Yash Tandon

ENDNOTES

1   Tandon, Yash (2015, 2017), *Trade is War*. OR-Books

2   On 7 April, 2017, Trump gave orders to his military to attack Syrian government air base on the grounds that from it Syria had launched chemical attacks on the rebels. This sent shock waves across the world. Russia issued a statement that this would undermine the peace effort, whilst the UK, Israel, Saudi Arabia and Australia supported the attack. At the time of writing this, it is early to assess Trump's motivation and the forces behind this action. In one of the pieces, I argue that although Trump is an anti-Establishment president, the "deep state" (including the military-industrial-financial complex), as well as close allies like Israel, Saudi Arabia, and the United Kingdom could push Trump on the course of war. I also said that the economies of these countries are unsustainable without the production and use of military hardware.

3   http://www.independent.co.uk/news/world/americas/us-elections/athletes-slam-donald-trump-locker-room-talk-excuse

4   https://www.theguardian.com/us-news/2016/nov/10/bernie-sanders-donald-trump-harnessed-anti-establishment-anger;
http://www.independent.co.uk/news/uk/politics/jeremy-corbyn-responds-to-donald-trump-win-america-election-hillary-clinton

5   See: Kathleen R. McNamara, "Trump takes aim at the European Union", Foreign Affairs, January 24, 2017. https://www.foreignaffairs.com/articles/europe/2017-01-24/trump-takes-aim-european-union

6   See: Tandon (2015), *Trade is War*, Chapter 6: From War to Peace - The Theory and Practice of Revolutionary Change.

7   http://www.bbc.co.uk/news/uk-politics-37966519

8   http://johnpilger.com/articles/inside-the-invisible-government-war-propaganda-clinton-trump

9   The day after the US elections, I received a circular from my friends at the Global Justice Network (GJN) - a justice oriented campaigning NGO - with who I am generally in agreement for 90 percent of the time. The circular started with the following: "We have woken up this morning to the most shocking news. An extreme nationalist has won the US presidential election on a campaign filled with racism, misogyny and hatred."

10 http://www.economist.com/news/21631966-bad-news-international-co-operation-nationalism-back

11 http://www.politifact.com/truth-o-meter/statements/2016/oct/19/hillary-clinton/hillary-clinton-blames-russia-putin-wikileaks

12 Polanyi, Karl (1957), *The Great Transformation. The Political and Economic Origins of our Times*, Beacon Press, 2001.

13 http://links.org.au/communist-manifesto-marx-engels-weapon-war-greene

14 http://www.pambazuka.org/en/category/features/91832

15 https://www.ft.com/content/b911380e-6e8a-11e5-8171-ba1968cf791a

16 See: Genevieve Ding, "The CNOOC Bid for Unocal and US National Security: Was the Political Outcry in Congress Justified?" https://sites.duke.edu/djepapers/files/2016/10/Ding.pdf

17 https://www.theguardian.com/business/2005/jul/21/usnews.france

18 See: Yuefen Li, "Implications of Argentina's Deal with 'Super holdouts'" http://www.alainet.org/es/node/175835

19 See: Ndletyana Mcebisi & David Maimele (eds.) 2014. *Resurgent Resource Nationalism*, Pretoria: MISTRA for an interesting study on this.

20 However, those interested in an ideological challenge to my views may want to read Sam Pryke's "Economic Nationalism: Theory, History and Prospects" *in Global Policy*, Vol. 3, Issue 2, September, 2012, where he makes the extraordinary claim that "the complexity of the global economy, makes it all but impossible to separate by nationality".

21 For an eye-opening account of this, see: Daniel Munevar, "*IMF explaining its own contribution in destroying South Europe*", where Munevar gives an account of the split within the political and technical divisions of the IMF that eventually ended with Germany using the IMF to protect the interests of German Banks. The IMF's Executive Board was kept in the dark, and told lies about what was taking place. The "Troika" (the IMF, the European Bank, and the European Commission) decided to give Greece more loans knowing fully well that the debt it was creating was unsustainable. This was mainly to protect German bonds that stood to lose €83 billion, and to give time to the Euro area to build firewall to prevent contagion. http://www.defenddemocracy.press/imf-explaining-its-own-contribution-in-destroying-south-europe

22 See, for example, Reinert, Erik S. Jayati Ghosh & Rainer Kattel, eds. 2016 Elgar Handbook of Alternative Theories of Economic Development

23 https://www.socialeurope.eu/2016/11/gold-plated-populism-trump-end-liberal-order

24 https://www.google.o.uk/#q=Trump%2C+in+Interview%2C+Moderates+Views+but+Defies+Conventions

25 Stephen Bannon (63) is described by many as a gifted thinker. He has had an unorthodox career. As a young man, he started out as a naval officer; then joined Goldman Sachs as a mergers specialist; then into documentary screen writing in the entertainment industry, etc. etc. He is a polymath.

26 http://www.bbc.co.uk/news/world-us-canada-38155141

27 http://johnpilger.com/articles/inside-the-invisible-government-war-propaganda-clinton-trump

28 http://fortune.com/2015/09/30/america-wealth-inequality/

29 http://talkingpointsmemo.com/livewire/where-sanders-may-work-with-trump

30 http://www.politico.eu/article/nato-chief-to-trump-going-alone-is-not-an-option

31 *https://www.google.co.uk/#q=Sunday+Times++War+With+Russia+%E2%80%9CTop+Ten+Bestseller%E2%80%9D*

32 http://www.globalresearch.ca/the-wages-of-u-s-imperialism-and-americas-war-machine/

33 http://www.globalresearch.ca/bankers-hate-peace-all-wars-are-bankers-wars/5438849

34 http://www.progressive.org/news/2014/05/187678/nomi-prins-speaks-out-why-she-bolted-wall-street

35 http://www.independent.co.uk/news/uk/politics/arms-sales-saudi-arabia-theresa-may-staunch-defence-keep-people-streets-britain-safe-a7230836.html

36 http://www.usatoday.com/story/news/world/2016/11/15/germans-bid-fond-farewell-obama-leery-trump

37 *https://www.thestar.com › News › World*

38　See https://en.wikipedia.org/wiki/Manifest_destiny

39　See: Timeline of United States government military operations. The list through 1775 is based on Committee on International Relations (now known as the House Committee on Foreign Affairs). https://en.wikipedia.org/wiki/Timeline_of_United_States_military_operations

40　See: Tim Shorrock Twitter https://www.thenation.com/article/how-hillary-clinton-militarized-us-policy-in-honduras/

41　On 18 November, British Prime Minister, Theresa May, vowed to keep pressure on Russia amid fears over Donald Trump's "alliance" with Vladimir Putin. On 23 November, *EU Parliament* approves *resolution - "At war with Russia"* - to counter alleged Russian propaganda *against* Europe. Of course, Obama, and with him, the entire US Establishment, have had ceaseless violent verbal attacks on Trump since Day One of the US elections, and still continuing.

42　https://www.theguardian.com/commentisfree/2016/nov/10/donald-trump-britain-greatest-fear-isolationist-president

43　https://www.theguardian.com/commentisfree/2016/nov/10/the-left-needs-a-new-populism-fast

44　Except for some enlightened individuals amongst them - historians like Karl Polanyi, philosophers like Jürgen Habermas, journalists like Chris Hedges, and solidarity organisations like the Geneva based CETIM - to mention those that come to my mind immediately.

45　You can get access to this essay in:kpolanyi.scoolaid.net:8080/xmlui/bitstream/.../Con_13_Fol_06%20 REVISED.pdf

46　See: https://www.researchgate.net/.../305418782_Sustaining_Democracy_

47　https://www.rt.com/uk/310448-cumbersome-democracy-russia-isis/ ... Queen Elizabeth's uncle, who became King Edward VIII, travelled to Nazi Germany in 1937 following his abdication. He was not only filmed giving Nazi salutes to Hitler, healso plotted with the Third Reich to form a Nazi-collaborationist regime in England.

48　Samir Amin, "The Return of Fascism in Contemporary Capitalism",Monthly Review, September 2014. https://archive.monthlyreview.org/index.php/mr/article/view/MR-066-04-2014-08

49　Roger Moody, (2007). Rocks and Hard Places: The Globalisation of Mining, Zed Press.

50　The same security firm is also deployed to guard oil and gas industry assets in war-torn Iraq.

51　See: Gaudiano, Nicole: "Bernie Sanders, Native Americans say oil pipeline will poison drinking water". USA Today, September, 13, 2016

52　Both Fukuyama and Huntington come from mainstream Western geopolitical and ideological thinking, based essentially on Eurocentric epistemologies. They boil down, in the case of Fukuyama, to a premature celebration of Western triumphalism at the end of the Cold War and the demise of the Soviet Union, and in the case of Huntington, to a fear of counter-Western civilizations, especially Islamic one. See Fukuyama (1992), *The End of History and the Last Man*, Free Press; and Huntington (1996), *The Clash of Civilizations and the Remaking of World Order*, Simon and Schuster.

53　See: "From War to Peace: The Theory and Practice of Revolutionary Change", in Tandon, Y. (2015), *Trade is War*, OR Books.

54　It is usual to contrast 'civilization' to supposedly barbarian or primitive cultures, such as those of hunter-gatherers and nomadic pastoralists. The word 'primitive' is highly pejorative and demeans many cultures – such as the Karamojong of Uganda, among whom I grew up as a child – that in many ways have a higher culture (in the sense of social bonding and peaceful means of internal conflict resolution) than our 'modern' industrial or post-industrial civilizations.

55　http://www.latimes.com/politics/essential/la-pol-ca-essential-politics-updates-calexit-organizers-say-they-ve-opened-1482187671-htmlstory.html

56 The "organic composition of capital" is the ratio of the value of the materials and fixed costs (constant capital) embodied in production of a commodity to the value of the labour-power (variable capital) used in making it.

57 See Part Two: "Imperialism and Revolution".

58 https://www.google.
co.uk/#q=Michael+Hudson:+The+Democracy+Collaborative.+Interviewed+by+Adam+Simpson

59 Sabelo J. Ndlovu-Gatsheni and & Finex Ndhlovu (eds), 2013. *Nationalism and National Projects in Southern Africa: New Critical Reflections*. Africa Institute of South Africa. https://www.pambazuka.org/resources/book-review-%E2%80%98nationalism-and-national-projects-southern-africa.